My Letters To Dead People: A Book You Should Write

By Richie Ross

1. Periodicals : Current Events - Politics 2. History : United States - State & Local - General 3. Biography & Autobiography : Personal Memoirs

ISBN: 978-1-935953-11-1

Cover Illustration and Design: Kathryn Storm

Letter Illustrations: Jeremy Clardy

Printed in the United States of America

Authority Publishing

11230 Gold Express Dr. #310-413

Gold River, CA 95670

800-877-1097

www.AuthorityPublishing.com

My Letters *to* DEAD PEOPLE

My Letters *to*
DEAD
PEOPLE

Richie Ross

Elias

By the time you

read thru you can

write me a letter

Richie

Foreword

Jonathan Shapiro

Richie Ross is a hard man to read.

He intends to be.

It's a job requirement.

He plays things close to the vest, never showing his cards; as a result, he has won as often with good hands as with bad ones.

For decades Ross has proven himself a champion in the art of political campaigning by blending boyhood Catholicism, 1960's idealism, New York moxie, and his transcultural Latino experiences.

Ross has been called many things, many of them profane. "Literary," "sensitive," and "intellectual" are not among them.

Ross has written a beautiful, wise, and thought-provoking book, one that has more in common with the essays of Michel de Montaigne or the Book of Ecclesiastes than the wise-guy sayings of Plunkett of Tammany Hall.

To call it merely a collection of letters to dead people is like calling St. Peter's letters just a bunch of church newsletters.

Each of these letters is a jewel.

They reflect lost lights and hidden history of the modern labor movement, the progressive movement in California, and the creation of our current political climate.

The letters are also filled with the most fascinating characters of the last fifty years. Some are known, others are unknown, but all are fully revealed, no one more so than Ross himself.

Montaigne wrote, "There is nothing so beautiful and legitimate as to play the man well and properly." Ross has done so, and this book explains how and why.

Richie Ross may be a hard man to read. But his book is anything but.

Dear Dad,

I never thought I would say that I was glad you were dead. But that's exactly what I was thinking on the morning of September 11, 2001.

When the news broke that morning, we all worried that Rob was working at his office in the World Trade Center.

Once I knew he was in Newark, my next thought was of you. And I was glad you were dead. I knew that if you saw those towers come down it would have broken your heart.

I remember when I was 14 and I started working as a messenger on Wall Street with you. It was back in the days when you were a clerk at Laird & Co. And for the next three summers I got to go to work with you every day.

You won't remember this, but the old men who were in charge of all the messengers used to look at my route and then tell me how long I should take. They didn't want me to hurry up—they wanted me to slow down. They said I was making the older guys look bad. They used to say, "Don't be a rate-breaker, kid." I had to ask you what they meant.

But I never slowed down. I used to pretend I was racing people on the sidewalk. I'd spot someone way ahead of me and then imagine I was a race car driver trying to beat him to the next corner. But after I'd finish my deliveries I would go kill time before going back to the office to get more. I had two favorite places.

My first place was the cemetery at Trinity Church on Broadway at the top of Wall Street. I would sit by the grave of Robert Fulton, who invented the steam engine. I would read the *Sporting News*.

The other place was the construction site for the World Trade towers.

What I remember most was how deep the hole was for the foundation. And you used to know so much about the buildings. Even how much steel they used. I never understood how you knew as much as you did. Or why it meant so much to you. Was it just your pride in the "Big Apple"?

When people attack the Yankees for spending more money on players, guys like us think they're either crazy or jealous. Like you always said, everything in New York was the best in the world. It's supposed to cost more.

You and I only had that one giant fight after I quit the seminary and you asked me about the draft. I told you I wasn't going to fight a corrupt war in Vietnam for a corrupt government in the United States. You told me you were going to get a gun and take me to the draft board.

I turned in my draft card and split for California. We didn't talk to each other for a couple of years. I tried to talk to you that one time when I came home to Staten Island. We were in the elevator when we lived over on Victory Boulevard. You wouldn't talk to me. We got off on the 10th floor; I followed you to our apartment. You went in and closed the door behind you.

After the World Trade towers got taken out by fucking terrorists flying hijacked airplanes into them, you and I would have agreed on going to war. I was so pissed off. And so was everyone in the whole country.

But leave it to the government...

Just like the Vietnam War and the Gulf of Tonkin, the government lied. This time it was about "weapons of mass destruction" that turned out not to exist, and we ended up going into Iraq instead of chasing the guilty bastards in Afghanistan and Pakistan.

But when you talk about father and son tensions, ours were nothing.

President Bush's son, George II, became president and he just couldn't resist trying to show up his old man after the first war in Iraq ended without us taking over Baghdad.

I wonder if you and I would have agreed about this. I bet we might have.

One thing I know we would have agreed on was how great it was that two of your grandchildren flew to New York to help after the attack.

Esperanza was working for the hotel and restaurant workers' union and she helped organize the memorial services for the workers who died at the Top of the World restaurant that day.

Joaquin hustled himself into volunteering as a truck driver delivering boots to the workers at Ground Zero. For weeks, the debris was so hot their boots would melt after just a few hours, so Joaquin re-supplied them.

Anyway, the politicians are still arguing about what the new building should look like.

But I think they've kind of agreed, and last time I was in New York a few months ago there was a lot of work going on below street level. I went to the same spot where I watched them build it the first time. It was weird.

Other than that, nothing is new.

Thanks for all you taught me. Especially about dying. The way you ended your dialysis after they cut off both your legs...

I will never forget our last conversation. You said, "I survived the big one and married my high school sweetheart."

I had to think about what you meant by the "big one."

It dawned on me as I walked away from the hospital that it was World War II and how I had no idea what you saw, experienced, thought or felt.

Love,
Richie

P.S. The Mets haven't done a thing since you died. The Giants won a Super Bowl on an unbelievable catch—guy goes up, makes a one hand grab and holds the ball against his helmet, hits the ground and never drops the ball.

Fr. Philip Berrigan
Baltimore, Maryland

Dear Father Berrigan,

I don't know if you remember me. I worked in your parish in Baltimore on weekends when I was in the seminary at St. Charles in Catonsville. You had me tutor little kids and help them with their homework.

I still remember walking behind you down the street. You

were carrying a little girl on your shoulders. You had really big shoulders.

I was one of the seminarians that you and your brother Daniel got into the anti-Vietnam War movement.

In fact, after you and he became the "Catonsville Nine" for burning the draft records, I went to NYU to meet with Daniel and some other young anti-war Catholics at the Jesuits' place on campus. We spent hours and hours talking and reflecting on what constitutes a person of conscience. If I am remembering right, I think we stayed up all night. Or at least almost all night.

I realized that Daniel was recruiting me for the next attack on a draft board. My classmate, Bill Au, signed up. I didn't. To be honest, I was afraid of going to jail. It's not that I'm ashamed of it. Well, maybe a little.

You had introduced me to Cesar Chavez the year before. And I felt like I had to do something big and important. Working with Cesar seemed both. It also felt safer than prison. I ended up getting arrested anyway, but nothing as serious or heavy as what you and your brother were doing.

I found in the farm workers' movement both a commitment to non-violence that matched Daniel's and a grounding in the realities of poor people's lives that matched the parish work I did with you.

But what I learned from Daniel has been with me ever since. He showed me how to understand things from the outside in, instead of from the inside out.

People are taught to think that outward actions are reflections of inner realities. By listening to Daniel, I came to understand that outward actions create inner realities. His poems weren't meant as expressions of himself but as inspirations for others.

Is the human embrace a reflection of warm feeling, or does it create the warm feeling it symbolizes?

Once I had this insight, I understood Catholic sacraments and the power of symbols to create what they symbolize.

From this I understood that your acts of civil disobedience were not expressions of your own beliefs but rather ways of creating disobedience in others.

Raising four children and a nephew I've come to realize that showing love for someone isn't an expression of love—instead, the expression creates the love itself.

I continue to work for the farm workers. And I enjoy it very much.

Thanks again. I remember you fondly.

Sincerely,
Richie Ross

Pete Hinton
Wilmington, Delaware

Dear Pete,

    I hope you're not dead. I hope you don't belong in this book.

    I haven't seen you since we were 19. A bunch of us visited you in the VA Hospital in Philadelphia after you stepped on a land mine in Vietnam.

We laughed with you about how one of your nuts got blown off. What the fuck were we thinking? That wasn't funny. But I guess we didn't know what else to do.

I felt the strain in our friendship.

You quit the seminary to join the Marines. I joined the anti-war movement. I didn't think you were wrong for what you decided was right. I felt bad knowing you thought I had betrayed our friendship when I made the opposite decision. In the seminary we always talked about wanting to help people and make the world better. But we ended up thinking differently about how to do that.

You put yourself in danger. The only danger I faced was pissing off my father by turning in my draft card.

When you would send us pictures from Vietnam, I could see that you were both brave and afraid. You always had a cigarette in the pictures. I smoked too much, too.

A few years after we lost contact with each other, I was in Washington, D.C. I decided to go to the Vietnam Veterans Memorial.

When it got built, I didn't understand the point of all of the names. But when I got there, I cried.

They built the memorial in about the same place we had a massive demonstration after Nixon started bombing the shit out of Cambodia.

It was creepy to be in the same place doing two very different things. Yelling back then; crying now.

I stared at all the names. You were the only person I knew who got hurt in Vietnam. But all the names of the dead guys seemed so familiar. It was like I was reading names of our classmates and neighborhood buddies. Ordinary names of ordinary guys like you.

I heard that after you got out of the hospital, you started drinking a lot. I didn't think it was a big deal. We used to drink a lot riding around Wilmington in that green Nash you had. I remember you pulling out a bottle of whiskey out from under the front seat. But I guess after the war you weren't drinking for fun.

I really wish we hadn't lost touch. There is so much we had in common. With time, I know that the anger you felt about me and the war would have gone away. I don't think you were really mad at me—just the whole thing. It messed us all up in a lot of ways.

If you are still alive, I hope you find this book of letters and maybe call me or find me on the Internet. I love you and would love to see you again…so I can take you out of the book.

Your friend,
Richie

Mr. Joe Chapman
Mother of the Savior Seminary
Blackwood, New Jersey

Dear Mr. Chapman,

You were the first person, other than Walter Cronkite, I
ever heard say the words "Vietnam War."
I was in your freshman English class in 1963.
There was some newspaper ad or poster or something that

you brought to class. It had a headline, "What price honor?" I don't remember much more. I was 14. But I remember how you wrote on the blackboard—which was green—"Why price honor?"

I can't tell you the point you were making. I can tell you I remember it was the first time anyone ever said that America was wrong about anything.

When I was little, I remember watching my father shave and asking him if we ever lost a war and if we were ever the bad guys. I was always happy when he told me "no." That happened a lot. I asked a lot. I liked hearing the answer a lot.

Then you said something different. And I'm glad you were my teacher.

If you don't mind, there are a few things I've learned about English from a lifetime in politics that you didn't teach me.

When a politician talks about how important loyalty is, that's the one who is going to fuck you. That happened to me.

When a politician tells you how good their word is—well, they're the liars. And of course, the ones who talk about morality or family values—they're doing some kinky bullshit.

Honest people don't talk about honesty. Strong people don't talk about strength. Tough guys don't talk about tough.

Point is, a life in politics is like being stuck on the movie set of the Wizard of Oz...the characters are all missing something...but they always tell you what it is by telling you what it isn't. Thanks for being a good teacher. Knowing now what no one knew then, your objections to the war were way ahead of the curve. I realize now you were being pretty brave.

Sincerely,
Richie Ross

HE STOOD HERE.

Man Standing on Broadway
American Express Building
New York, New York

Dear Sir,

The first time I saw you was the first day I ever worked at a job. I was 14. I was starting a summer job as a messenger boy on Wall Street. My dad was a clerk. He helped me get the job.

Walking up Broadway, he pointed you out to me.

"See that man? Over there standing on the subway grate? He's been standing there for years. He doesn't bother anybody. He comes at 9:00. He takes an hour for lunch. He leaves at 5:00. He's there every day. Rain. Snow. He reads his paper. You'll see him there every day."

When I asked my father why you did it, he told me he heard some company in the American Express Building fired you and that you were protesting it or something.

Where I worked, the other messengers were old. And they told me, "Don't make waves." And when I asked what they meant by that one guy explained, "Life is like swimming in water with lots of seagull shit. So you don't make waves. Because you don't want seagull shit in your mouth." I guess you made waves.

I'd walk by you six or seven times a day as a messenger. And I did it for three summers. I even took friends who visited New York to see you. You were part of my tour.

You were the first protester I ever saw in person. It was way before the anti-war movement.

When I was 17, I understood you better.

When I would pick up my messenger deliveries it was through a "cage"—an old-fashioned bank window. I could see where my dad sat, in the middle of a giant group of other clerks. Everyone processing stock trades by hand. With pencils.

One day, my dad's desk was gone. He was sitting on a folding chair. His phone was on the floor. And he had stacks of paper all around him.

That night as we walked down Broadway to the Staten Island Ferry, I asked him what was up. He told me they had given him his two-week notice. He was being fired. After twenty-some years.

I didn't know what to say. I didn't say anything.

16

I heard him talking to my mom that night.

The next day, we got up for work as usual. We read *The Daily News* on the ferry. He had his coffee. I ate my orange Hostess cupcakes.

I was ashamed for him. And a little ashamed of him. I hated how he just worked through his last two weeks like that.

Summer ended during his last week. I went back to the seminary. I was glad I could run away with a good reason.

My dad got a job as a night watchman at the Gulf Oil refinery in New Jersey. He struggled there. He had to move my mom and three younger brothers to a cheaper apartment. He never talked about it.

It took him five years of bouncing around from job to job before Merrill Lynch gave him a clerk job. He was so happy. He loved putting on his shirt and tie and going to work.

I came to appreciate what you did.

I should have stopped and talked to you.

Sincerely,
Richard Ross

Fr. William Lee
President
St. Mary's Seminary
Baltimore, Maryland

Dear Father Lee,

   The last hour I spent with you changed my life in more ways than any other hour of my life.

   I was nervous about coming to see you. I knew you were angry with me. You had given me so much freedom. And I abused it.

You always made sure I had time to be with both Fathers Daniel and Philip Berrigan. You never objected to the classes I skipped after Cesar Chavez asked me to run the Grape Boycott in Baltimore.

But when I organized the three-day march for the farm workers from Baltimore to Washington, I never showed up for class. Ever.

I knew I needed to come see you. I knew you would yell at me.

But you didn't.

Instead you said that I needed to "take a year off and go to Delano."

I couldn't believe it! I was relieved, happy, and nervous.

You warned me that if I did, I probably would never return to the seminary. Never become a priest.

That part scared me.

I never remembered wanting to be anything other than a priest. From the time I was very small. I thought it made me my mother's favorite son and the apple of my father's eye.

How would I tell them? What would they say? Should I tell them the part about how you thought I wouldn't come back? Or just the part about how you thought it was a good idea for me to go for a year?

I ended up lying and told them you had arranged for me to live with a group of priests in Delano. Chicken. I chickened out.

A couple of weeks after I got to Delano in the summer of 1970, there was a huge strike in the Salinas Valley and Cesar told us all to go there.

Me and two other guys drove that night. It took us four or five hours, I can't remember. We got lost.

When we got to Salinas we were hungry. A new Round Table Pizza place had opened that day. We went in and split a large pepperoni.

We walked around the corner to the old storefront the union had rented for the strike headquarters. We could see through the big windows that people were sleeping on the floor.

We knocked on the glass but no one could hear us.

So while one of the guys waited in front, two of us went around back and jumped over a fence so we could bang on the back door.

Just as someone came to open the back door, we heard our buddy, Doug, yelling at the front door. He was actually screaming. We ran and opened the front door. It was dark, but we could see he was getting beat up by some guys.

We ran out to help. Then more guys jumped us.

I got whacked in the head and started bleeding; then I was handcuffed; then I was in the back of a cop car; then I was in the police station; then I was getting punched and yelled at for not being able to get my driver's license out fast enough even though I was handcuffed; then I was being charged with assaulting a cop.

Wow. What a place. What a night. Pardon my French, Father Lee, but how fucked up was this?

The next day we got out of jail when the United Farm Workers' lawyers came for us.

But over the next three weeks I was involved in a high-speed car chase on Highway 101...I watched a guy aim a rifle at Cesar Chavez when we were picketing...and I got sent to the hospital when I got caught trying to get into a farm labor camp in a small town called King City.

These goon guys knocked me down and kicked the shit out of me and broke two or three ribs.

When Cesar Chavez saw me the next day he asked me if I was all right. I told him I was, and then he sent me back. He told me to go back to the camp after dark that night. He gave me the name of a "Chavista" (a supporter of the Union) and told me to find this guy and he would get the other farm workers together to help me.

The first time I went to that labor camp I was too stupid to be scared. This time I knew enough to be scared.

I parked my little car down a dirt road and slid under a part of the chain-link fence where there was a gully. Then I crawled underneath the bathroom and kitchen building. Around it were tiny little one-room bungalow cabins.

A lady came out of the kitchen with a pot of food she cooked and I asked her, "*Donde está Simón Trujillo?*"

The lady pointed to one of the cabins.

I knocked on the door. A man let me in. The room was crowded with other men. Simón knew a little English and between us I was able to get the information Cesar wanted.

There was only a single light bulb hanging from a wire in the middle of the cabin. It was dim. I didn't want to stare. But I could see lots of little kids squeezed onto a couple of bunk beds, watching our meeting.

Simón and the men walked with me back to my car. They had heard about what happened to me the day before. And they didn't want me to get hurt again.

I remember noticing Simón was carrying a small suitcase.

When we reached my car he put the suitcase on the back seat. Behind him in the dark was a girl. As she got closer to the car, I could see she was my age and very pretty.

Simón said that I should take her to Cesar because she was "joining *la revolución*."

Much changed in my life. I married that girl a year later. We had four children and raised a nephew.

Father, I never forgot you or your wisdom. And I've prayed often that I could be that wise with my own children.

God bless you. And peace.
Richie Ross

Larry Itliong
Delano, California

Dear Larry,

I thought you'd enjoy this story.
I was doing a union campaign for hotel housekeepers in
Honolulu in 2008. All of the women in the meeting were
Filipinas.
I was trying to figure out some messaging for the

campaign. Out of the blue I asked a crazy question. Don't even know why I did.

"If you had a big problem in your life, would you pray to God, to Jesus, or to the Blessed Mother?"

The ladies all looked at one another with a little smile. Finally, one of them asks me a question.

"When you boy, you have best friend?"

"Yes, I had a best friend."

"When you at best friend's house, did best friend ever make you one sandwich?"

"No, he didn't."

"But his mother made you sandwich, no?"

"Yeah, she did."

"So you see, Jesus may be your best friend, but if you need something you go to his mother."

We all laughed. I got the point. We continued the meeting.

Flying home, I was thinking about things.

I thought of you.

The first time I ever saw the word "Filipino" was when I arrived in Delano and was sent to sleep on the floor with all the other volunteers in Filipino Hall.

You woke me up my first morning there, tapping me with your boot. I looked up and saw you with your unlit cigar in your hand with two fingers chopped off. You had those glasses with big black frames.

"Let's go, Richard. I'm Larry. You're my driver. And you're taking me and Dolores to Salinas to meet with Cesar."

Driving you was the first time I saw how beautiful California was. I had hitchhiked straight to Delano from New York and was pretty disappointed with what California looked like. No palm trees. No beaches. Just poor people, little run-down houses and big trucks parked all over the place. And people had chickens. I couldn't believe it. Fucking chickens. I thought chickens were supposed to be on farms, not in people's yards.

You and Dolores argued and talked all the way to Salinas. We actually met Cesar at the Franciscan Monastery near San Juan Bautista. Listening to you all plan the Salinas strike was really something. It was the first time I had ever been in a meeting like that. It felt like a movie.

After that trip, you kept me as your driver. I learned a lot from you when we went to the labor camps where the Filipino workers lived. Sometimes you made me wait for a while when you visited a lady.

I didn't know that it was you who started the grape strike in Delano with the Filipino workers and that Cesar and the Mexican workers actually joined "your" strike. I tell people that fact all the time, because people should know.

After the vegetable strike in Salinas I never saw you again. But I never forgot you either. Cesar died. Dolores is still kicking.

Richie

P.S. Maybe it was because the old Filipino guys who cooked for us in Filipino Hall didn't have much to work with, but I never developed a taste for Filipino food.

Frank Rizzo
Mayor of Philadelphia

Dear Asshole,

You're dead. I'm not.

You were such a fucking creep when you were police chief, I can't believe that decent people would elect you mayor.

I was just a kid. Right out of the seminary. Running the farm workers' lettuce boycott. We lived on Masher Street near Kensington in North Philly.

Every morning we all got up at 4:00, got in our freezing cold car and headed for the produce market so we could see which stores were buying lettuce we were boycotting.

And every fucking morning you had your fucking cops pull us over, trash our car and throw all our shit all over the street. In the rain, in the snow, in the shitty slush.

Then your fucking cops arrested the young farm worker girl we had with us after some asshole at the produce market turned a water hose on us in the freezing winter. She went around behind him, jumped on his back, turned the hose around on him and knocked him on his fucking ass.

Then when I went downtown to try and bail her out, one of your jerk cops grabbed me and threw me on my ass. For nothing, you fucking fuck.

You, the cops in Salinas who beat me up, none of you were enforcing the law. You were using badges and guns to protect an America that never was. Ozzie and Harriet was a fucking TV show, you stupid fuck.

Richard Ross

Saul Alinsky
Carmel, California

Dear Mr. Alinsky,

A few years after you died, I invited myself to go visit Mrs. Alinsky. I found your house in Carmel. I was nervous. But not scared. I was a New Yorker. And I had been trained by some of your top protégés—Fred Ross and Cesar Chavez. So I walked up to your front door and knocked. Your wife answered. I introduced myself to her.

I explained that I was a "student" of yours and that Fred and Cesar had trained me as an organizer. Your wife invited me in.

We sat down in your living room. I explained that I had read your books a bunch of times and I knew you had been working on another book when you died. I had heard it was going to be about the importance and power of organizing shareholders to influence corporate behavior in America.

She listened.

I talked about what I had learned from *Reveille for Radicals* and *Rules for Radicals.* She let me tell her a few stories about things I had done with what I had learned from your books.

Mrs. Alinsky liked this one story I told her about a huge concert in Philadelphia and how we got Joan Baez to announce that the farm workers had started a lettuce boycott (after the Grape Boycott was over).

Mrs. Alinsky said it reminded her of something you would have done. That made me feel proud.

She told me to follow her. We went into your study. Your desk was piled with papers. She picked up some well-used spiral notebooks. She handed them to me and said I could sit and read them.

She warned me that your handwriting wasn't good and the notes weren't in any real order.

For the next two hours I read your notebooks. I sat in your chair. I felt like I was really listening to you talk. Even though I never heard you speak. I think it was because I was reading your handwriting. It was great.

I went back out to the kitchen and asked her if it was okay if I wrote some notes of my own. She smiled and told me that she'd prefer that I didn't. Of course, I agreed and went back to your desk.

No one ever really followed through on your book's premise. There's been some small stuff here and there. Some unions have used shareholder democracy to leverage stuff. Some consumer groups have tried things.

But it never really took hold in the way that other things have. Community organizing is still alive and well. Many of the organizing tactics, strategies and rules that you developed in Chicago are still in practice today. Hell, I still use them in my union work once in a while.

Corporate governance ran amok. It ultimately led to more and more deregulation and—no surprise to you—eventually it brought on what we called the "Great Recession."

Millions of people lost their jobs. Millions lost their homes. The government had to step in and bail out banks and GM. But even then, corporations went back to business as usual.

I wish more people had the chance I did. Maybe if folks read your notebooks. Or maybe if you had lived a few more years. Maybe things would have turned out better than they did.

Your wife was nice. She made me tea. I drank it in your kitchen. And I remember what I read that day.

Sincerely,
Richie Ross

Woody Guthrie
America

Dear Mr. Guthrie,

   Martin Scorsese made a great documentary about Bob
Dylan. I know...you're thinking, who are they? Both pretty
famous...after your time.
   Bob Dylan modeled himself after you. He studied all your
music. And over time, he became the poet of my generation.

I thought about your "Joe Hill" song and thought you'd enjoy this story.

After Cesar Chavez won the grape boycott, there was a giant vegetable strike in California. It led to the Lettuce Boycott.

I was sent to Philadelphia to run the boycott there.

Some nice supporters of the United Farm Workers donated a dozen tickets to a Joan Baez concert for all of the boycotters to go. We were pretty excited. We didn't ever get to do that kind of thing—we didn't have any money. Cesar Chavez only paid us $5.00 a week. So after cigarettes and beer, there wasn't any money for movies or concerts or anything else. Maybe a pizza once in a while.

The concert was at the Spectrum, which was the big arena in Philadelphia. It's torn down now.

It was a really big place. And Joan Baez was a really big performer in 1970, so she sold it out.

We thought it would be cool if we could get her to announce there was a new farm workers boycott. So we came up with this crazy idea that we'd bring a crate of grapes with the United Farm Workers Union Label on them and try to give them to Ms. Baez.

I wrote a letter on the top of the crate thanking her for supporting Cesar and the Grape Boycott and telling her about the new Lettuce Boycott.

We carried the grapes into the Spectrum and up to our seats in the nosebleeds.

After the concert got going, I took a very pretty farm worker girl, who was a boycotter with us, down the stairs. I carried the grapes. We walked to the edge of the stage. I told the security guard we were with Cesar Chavez and we were supposed to have this farm worker girl give the grapes to Ms. Baez at a certain point in the concert.

He bought it.

A song or two later, I slide the crate of grapes onto the stage and give the girl a boost up. She picks up the box and walks right up to the stool where Joan is sitting and singing.

At first, Joan was startled. Then she read the letter on the box and told the girl to stand there on stage while she dedicated her next song to the farm workers movement.

"I dreamed I saw Joe Hill last night..."

It was a really great moment. The crowd went crazy.

Sincerely,
Richie Ross

P.S. Joan Baez just sent the farm workers a financial contribution the other day.

Cesar Chavez
United Farm Workers
Keene, California

Dear Cesar,

Do you remember when we got drunk in your house? It was after the Ed Bradley interview for 60 Minutes.

We had worked so hard preparing. We were all so nervous. Marc and I worried that you'd make a mistake. You had been getting pounded in the press for so long.

The whole union was down to just a few people left. People today forget or have no idea.

Looking back I think about how we survived. How we kept going. And yes, I do remember getting drunk with you. It was so crazy. First of all, I never saw you drink. And second, I never saw Helen so mad as she was the next morning.

Anyway, I wanted to tell you a kind of funny story about what happened right after you died.

I didn't know what you were doing in Arizona. Marc came into my office in Sacramento with a sick look on his face and said you had died in your sleep.

It wasn't until after the funeral that I found out you were in Arizona because we were on trial for some shit I had helped you do when we were fighting the Bruce Church Lettuce Co.

I actually didn't know how much trouble the union was in and how it was because of what you and I had done.

Anyway, the guys call me and tell me I was the only witness the union had to defend itself. So they told me I had to come to Arizona.

Holy shit. It was a mess. Our lawyer was crazy Mike Aguirre. I shouldn't call him crazy. He was only crazy because he agreed to jump in and help us. He was smart. Just a little crazy, like the rest of us. And he was volunteering, just like the rest of us. And just like he had a lot of other times. But still, he was crazy.

We were all holed up in the little farm worker motel. Mike had piles of paper and shit all over one room that he turned into his "office." That was where he was going to prepare me to testify.

He went over the facts of the case...over and over. He told me what kind of questions they had been asking you and what they would be asking me.

I tried to remember things. But it was hard.

Today, I can remember going to a bar at night after every day of prep and I'd watch the Phoenix Suns and the Chicago Bulls in the playoffs.

Finally, Mike thought I was ready...and ready or not, the judge was starting up the trial again.

The courtroom was right out of the movies. I felt like I was in *To Kill a Mockingbird*. Ceiling fans turning slowly. Pissed-off white guy jurors. Frowning judge. Hostile prosecutor. And me.

You'd laugh at how many times they would remind me— "Let me remind you, Mr. Ross, you are under oath."

I guess they thought I would lie to protect the union from losing everything it had to a giant, asshole lettuce grower. Who—by the way—I had once worked for when I needed money, and I got on a crew thinning lettuce with a short-handle hoe and got fired after three days because I couldn't keep up with the crazy speed they made everyone work. So why would I lie?

The best part came when they asked me about where we would meet to plan out the campaign against Bruce Church. I don't know if you even remember. It was in that Chinese restaurant upstairs on that old street in San Jose. For whatever reason, the judge or the prosecutor asked me the name of the place. I couldn't remember. Royal Dragon or some shit. So I told them I thought it was called Food Nice.

Some people in the courtroom laughed. Even a couple of the pissed-off white guys on the jury smiled. But the judge didn't think it was funny. And he yelled at me, "because this was no laughing matter."

No laughing matter. That's what the nuns at St. Ladislaus in New Brunswick used to tell me. "This is no laughing matter, young Mr. Ross."

"Yes, Sister."

"Yes, your Honor."

Fuck you guys.

Anyway, I was on the witness stand for a pretty long time. Dolores came with a lot of farm workers and sat in the courtroom. It was good to see her out there.

I think we lost in that court but eventually we won on appeal.

Artie continues to do a great job as president. Paul finished the north unit at La Paz and it's now a great learning center. You should see it. When Helen cut the ribbon a few weeks ago, Paul honored my daughter Esperanza for playing a key role in getting the project funded. So it was kind of a special day for me. Your son finishing your project with my daughter helping. Good shit.

After the ceremonies, we had a meeting to plan the union's 50th anniversary. My son Joaquin had made a video about the union's history. He did a better job than he did right after you died and I sent him down to La Paz to help Artie by being his driver. It didn't work out so good. He smashed up your car, which had become Helen's car. The video was better.

Your gravesite in La Paz is beautiful. I know you're resting in peace.

We all continue the work. And it goes well.

Si se puede,
Richie

Tony
Staten Island, New York

Dear Tony,

I figure that you ended up the way most wise guys do...
dead or in prison.

Anyway, I wanted to write to thank you for getting me out
of the restaurant business.

Maybe you remember me. I had the new Mexican

restaurant over by the ferry terminal across from Richmond Community College. It was called Montezuma's.

You came in one afternoon. You sat at the counter and asked me where my cigarette machine was. When I told you that I didn't sell cigarettes but the deli on the corner did, you smiled and told me that this was my lucky day. You were in the cigarette machine "business."

Yeah, right.

I knew who you were. And that you had connections. So, I knew I was going to accept your generous "offer."

The next day, you brought the cigarette machine in. Fifty cents a pack. And once a week you'd come, open up the money box and we'd split the quarters. What could I say? You just did it. Seemed like a fair deal.

I noticed the cigarettes had no tax stamp on the bottom of the packs. So I knew they weren't exactly kosher. Hey, my grandfather was a "buttlegger." He had a route around Wall Street and he sold cartons of cigarettes for $2.40. So I knew how it worked.

A couple of weeks later you asked me how I could expect to be doing business with "that Puerto Rican crap" music we had playing in the place. I explained that it was Mexican music and this was a Mexican restaurant. Don't know if you knew this, but we were like one of the first ones in the city. Now they're all over the place and no one complains about the music. But you said "regular" people weren't going to enjoy their meal because this Puerto Rican music would give them heartburn. You said it gave you heartburn.

You "invited" me to this house and said I could pick out a nice jukebox and even the records it would play. What a fucking deal!

"You can mix it up. Some Frank. Some Tony Bennett. And if you want some of that Spanish stuff, you can have that, too. Give people a choice. You don't just have one dish on your menu, so have a music menu. I'm telling you, people will love it. They love it. And we'll split the money, just like the cigarettes."

Things went fine. I told the restaurant's real owner, Luke Kauffman, that we were making money. I was just his working partner.

And shit, it was Staten Island in 1972. The cops on the beat would come in and eat for free. They wouldn't even come to the cash register and offer to pay. They'd just walk out when they were done eating. So what if I didn't like doing business with you, Tony? Gonna call the cops? They were your cops.

We put up some new awnings. They were metal ones. Gave the front of the place a nice look. The business was starting to do pretty good.

You came in and told me that I should get some insurance on them. Because you said the wind might blow them down.

When I told Mr. Kauffman, he said no way was he going to pay insurance. So I told you. And sure enough, must of have been one fucking strong gust of wind because I came down on Sunday to get things ready for the next week and the "wind" had knocked the awnings down and smashed them. Never knew the wind could make a metal awning look like it had been smashed with a bat.

But you know what, Tony? You did me a favor. I hated the restaurant. We were there from 5:00 in the morning to 11:00 at night. It was like being in jail. I thought it was going to be something different. I had a stupid idea that I was going to get rich. My plan was to buy hot dog carts and sell tacos off them. Even though no one in New York even knew what a taco was. I had my head up my ass.

But your little insurance program changed everything. Mr. Kauffman sold the place.

I flew my family back to California. I stayed behind to

finish painting a bank. I was painting on the side. But once it was done, I loaded everything we had into our Chevy Vega and drove back to California.

I bet a bunch of guys I worked with, when I drove a garbage truck, $100 that I could make it to California in 40 hours. The whole trip. Start to finish, 40 hours. They would know if I did it because our plan was that I would call them collect from a pay phone. So then the operator would ask them if they'd accept a collect call from me in Salinas, California. There weren't cell phones then.

I made it. The guys sent me the money. And that's how I paid for the gas.

Sincerely,
Richie Ross

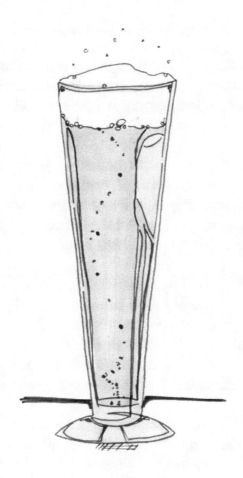

Frank Ross
Brooklyn, New York

Dear Chief,

 I never did understand where you got that nickname.
Uncle Mel was the one who always used it. He said you were
the chief of the family. I guess. But since this letter is about
our names...
 Me first.

You'll love this. I get my first job in a politician's office and after a week, one of the guys there tells me I really ought to change my name. "Richie makes you seem like a kid. Did you ever consider using Dick?"

Dick!

When we lived in the South Beach projects I had to fight kids who called me "Dick." And then, when I got Confirmation, I took my best friend's first name to be my Confirmation name. He was Peter Mulroy. So that made me "Dick Peter." You can imagine how much crap I took for that.

Dick!

The guy wasn't kidding. I didn't know whether to laugh or shit. But I'd just started with these guys so I kept my mouth shut, kept my job, but kept my name.

Your name story is better than mine.

Frankie D'Ambrosia. Now, that's a cool name. I would've grown up as "Richie D." And that would have been really cool.

When Dad died we found the court papers from 1953 when you actually changed your name to Frank Ross. We never knew that wasn't always your name.

Uncle Mel had told us a long time ago that you had changed our dad's name to Frank Ross in the 1930s when the nuns wouldn't let him into St. Teresa's Grammar School as Frankie Ross, since the name on his birth certificate was Francis D'Ambrosia.

After you died, we asked ourselves if we should change our name back to D'Ambrosia.

But then we learned that you really were Frankie Ross. In a very Brooklyn way.

Mom told us you delivered bread to all the stores in Flatbush and the bakery's name was "Ross." So you got nicknamed "Frankie the Ross," and so Dad was Frankie the Ross' kid, Frankie Ross.

Wild.

We discussed it one Sunday afternoon but ended up deciding we weren't really that Italian. Mom was Irish/ English. And we really were more from Brooklyn than from some other country. So keeping a real Brooklyn name, I mean really from Brooklyn, seemed like the best thing to do.

Rejecting "Dick" was a lot easier decision.

Love,
Richie

P.S. We all still remember the last time you took us "bouncing" through all your hangout bars in Brooklyn.

Jim Herman
President
International Longshore and Warehousemen's Union

Dear Jim,

You grew up in New Jersey. So you'd get this...
I'd start every baseball season buying two packs of baseball cards.

I was short. Like you. And couldn't hit a baseball. But I'd

take my baseball cards to St. Ladislaus every day.

Remember flippsies? One kid would flip a card, then I'd flip a card. If his landed heads up and then mine did, both cards were mine.

Topsies was better because you could win more, faster. We'd take turns flipping cards at the wall. When someone's card landed on top of another card, they won all the cards on the ground.

But my favorite was knocksies. Sometimes we called it leansies. We'd lean a card against the wall and take turns flipping cards at it. Whoever knocked the leaning card down won all the cards. These pots got really big.

There were two kinds of kids. Some wanted to play for funsies. Some for keepsies. At the end of the baseball season I always had a shoebox full of cards. Didn't care which players were on them. Just wanted a full box.

Whenever I go to the United Airlines terminal at the San Francisco airport, I remember that night when we were playing for keepsies. Two a.m. You call me to pick you up at 2nd and Berry Streets. I just figured you had a late meeting or something.

I jumped into that '72 Plymouth Fury you bought for me to drive you around in when you were campaigning to succeed Harry Bridges as president of the ILWU.

(I still remember the time you were campaigning in front of a big crowd of the longshore guys in the Local 6 hall. Some guy stood up and called you a "four-eyed little fuck" and said you would sell the guys out to the companies.

The hall was crowded. The guys were all drinking beer and whatever.

I couldn't see your eyes from where I was standing when the guy attacked you, but I could tell you didn't blink.

You just grabbed the microphone and attacked him back by telling everyone that you saw him on the sidewalk talking to one of the bosses. "What were you talking about? The secret deal you tried to make to sell all of us out? You're a fucking liar and a whore."

The whole crowd started to turn on the guy. Then you shouted, "Get the fuck out of here. And don't come back."

When we got back in the car I said, "Wow, Mr. Herman, I thought politics was rough. Lucky you caught the guy talking to the boss on the sidewalk. That really got him."

"I didn't," was all you said. Then you laughed. And I thought to myself, "Holy shit.")

Anyway, back to the night when you called for me to come get you. …

When you stepped out of that doorway on Second Street and got into the car, I could tell something was up and it wasn't good. You asked me if a silver Chevy was following us. I told you I couldn't tell what color the car behind us was. You said, "Turn right." I did. The car followed. "Turn right again, kid."

"They're still behind us."

"Lose them! Go up on the freeway! Let's go."

My leg was shaking so bad I had a hard time keeping the gas pedal all the way down. The car had a 440-cubic-inch engine in it and really shitty suspension. We were flying. Really fucking flying. And bouncing. Felt like we were going to bounce right off the freeway.

"Where do we go, Mr. Herman?"

"To the airport."

"I don't see them behind us."

"Just drive. Pull up in front of the United terminal and leave the car. We gotta be in a public building."

"Won't we get towed?"

"Doesn't matter."

I bring up this whole story because when the sun came up and we got the car back, you told me to come over to your house so we could go eat breakfast together. You wanted to show off your new, used Mercedes 280SL.

You took me for a spin. Then we hung a tennis ball on a string in your garage so you would know to stop when it touched your windshield. Your eyes were so bad that not even the thickest glasses in the world could keep you from bumping into the wall.

At breakfast, I asked you what I should do with the strongbox if something ever happened to you.

"You'll know what to do," was all you said.

We knew something important was in the box after you had me build that fake wall in our house to hide it. But it wasn't until those guys tried to kill us or whatever that night, that I realized it must be really, really important.

I never asked. You never said. You'd just call us every month or so and say the code words "I'm coming over to see the kids." I'd drag that heavy box out of its hiding place and take the real kids out for a walk.

I know we're not supposed to talk about it, even now. But hell, no one's gonna kill you, Jim. You're already dead.

I confess to wondering not just about what was in the box, but what I was supposed to do with it if something ever happened to you. Even though you said I would figure it out, I was always trying to figure it out. I'm always figuring out shit.

It wasn't until Art and Sherry had us all over to their house to celebrate your 70th birthday after you retired. Had to be 20 years later. Art reached into his wallet and pulled out a key.

"Jim, you asked me to hold this key years ago. What was it for?"

You looked at me. Then you said, "I think it was for an old locker or something. I forget."

Jim, thanks for all you did for me. All the places you took

us. You taught us how to eat in nice restaurants and use the right fork. I even have the tie you shoplifted for me in Carmel.

We're sad you died. But glad it was from old age.
We all send our love.

Richie

P.S. I drove your Mercedes 280SL up to Lake Tahoe. That's right. It's 40 years old and still runs and looks great and I still have it.

Harvey Milk
San Francisco, California

Dear Harvey,

I feel like such a chicken-shit.

They made a movie about you. I haven't gone to see it. And won't.

You aren't expecting an apology; you don't even know about the movie or who Sean Penn is. He plays you.

All the reviews said he did a great job. When I saw the advertisements, it was weird how much he resembled you.

Cleve Jones was heavily involved in the project for years and he made sure that *Milk* was true to your story.

After you were killed, Cleve came to work with me in Art Agnos' office. We became pretty good buddies. But we lost touch with each other after I went to work for Willie Brown.

When the whole AIDS thing was so out of control, Cleve created the AIDS Memorial Quilt. It ended up memorializing 50,000 or more people who had died from the disease. I'm convinced the government response to the crisis grew in proportion to his quilt. You'd have been proud.

A few years ago, Cleve went to work for the hotel workers' union. I've been working with them for 25 years. So it was really great to reconnect with him just as the movie was being released. It was neat to listen to him tell stories about the project and all he did to get the movie made. Tons of people have gone to see it and you'd enjoy listening to the young, straight kids talk about marriage equality which is pretty close to happening.

So anyway, I haven't gone to see *Milk*.

I feel funny about it after running Art's campaign against you for state Assembly in 1976.

Your "Harvey Milk vs. The Machine" campaign was really brilliant. Our campaign had everything a "machine" has— money, endorsements, all of it. You ran on a shoestring.

At the time, it was all about survival for me, a roof over my wife and kids' head. But for you, it was about something much bigger. Looking back, I know that now.

We had been living in a small hotel just north of the Tenderloin. We had two kids living in a tiny room. I got free rent by working as the night clerk.

Art had picked me up hitchhiking and offered me a job in a political campaign. I wasn't even registered to vote. I was like you but maybe more lefty...one of those new-left anti-war kids. The ones who gave the correct answer to the posters that asked, "What if they gave a war and nobody came?" We didn't go. And because we didn't, Nixon had to "officially" end the whole fucking thing.

But my sense of political empowerment crashed into the reality of having kids but not any money. It sucked. I went one time to get food stamps. You know what that's like? Ain't pretty. Ever been to a "free" clinic? It's not free of humiliation.

When I asked my dad what he thought I should do when Art offered me a job in the "political establishment" he said, "Play ball with these guys, Richie." So I did.

And that put you and me on a collision course. Because you weren't about "playing ball"; you were about starting a movement.

I feel bad today about running around the city at night, tearing down your campaign signs. At the time it was fun. Me and another guy would spot one of your signs on a telephone pole, pull over, he'd squat down, I'd climb on his shoulders, he'd stand up, and I'd tear down your sign. What the fuck, Harvey. Didn't your guys ever figure out that they needed to put 'em up another two or three feet and you'd have won the sign war?

But it was like we were being the bullies. And I hate bullies.

But the bright side was that your unsuccessful campaign for Assembly set you up to win your seat on the board of supervisors. The downside is it set you up to get killed. And that shouldn't have happened. And you wouldn't have gotten killed if you had beaten us and gone into the state Assembly instead of City Hall with that nut Dan White.

I confess not to have seen the historic significance of your win at the time. Not because I didn't think about it. It's just that there were so many historic things happening that none of us really could appreciate what they all would come to mean. Or that some would be bigger than others. The environmental movement. The women's movement. The civil rights movement. The gay rights movement. Lots of things moving. And we called them all "movements." All part of the "Movement."

If you weren't a movement or part of one, you weren't shit.

I loved and hated you at the same time. Loved that you were an irreverent New Yorker challenging the establishment. Hated that you might derail my new job.

But none of this stuff is the reason I can't see your movie.

Enclosed is a copy of my letter to Mayor Moscone. I know he wouldn't mind me sharing it with you. I hope after reading it, you'll understand better.

All the best,
Richie

P.S. That 1977 campaign picture of you standing in front of your camera shop, smiling, with your tie blowing in the wind, is one of the best political photos ever. It's in the California Museum. Glad you didn't use it in 1976.

Mayor George Moscone
San Francisco, California

Dear Mayor Moscone,

I am writing to thank you for considering appointing me to the board of supervisors.

I know that when Dan White resigned his seat and then asked you to re-appoint him because he changed his mind, you were inclined to do it. Everyone said that you were that kind of guy.

But you made the right political decision to not re-appoint White. Your re-election wasn't looking good. You were on the losing side of a 6-5 conservative majority on the board of supervisors, and the White vacancy gave you a chance to flip it the other way.

When Art Agnos and Leo McCarthy told me you were willing to consider me for the appointment to the White seat, I was flattered, honored, and tempted.

As it turned out, I'm glad I decided against pursuing it.

We had been so poor for so long that I just couldn't see how it made sense to take a $7,000 pay cut to become a supervisor. I don't know if you knew this, but before getting my job with Art and Leo, I had worked in the fields around Salinas. I cut broccoli, lettuce, and cauliflower. I picked strawberries, too. It was so hard that I would get a fever every night. I cried a lot of days. I was so frustrated that I couldn't get out and get something better. I got drunk once and shoved a beer bottle through our apartment wall.

After I said I wasn't interested, Art asked me to get you guys someone else. I thought of Don Horanzy. He was a buddy of mine who worked in the neighborhood where we both lived in the Outer Mission. I think we became friends because he was married to a Filipina and I was married to a Mexican.

On the morning you were going to appoint Don, he and his family were over in Art's assembly office in the State Building. We were having a little breakfast reception for him and his family. His family was so proud. Everyone was all dressed up.

That's when we heard the sirens...and then the news.

It's terrible to say this, but all I could think of at the moment was how horrible it would have been if it was my family there, all dressed up waiting for me to get sworn in that morning in your office.

I'm sorry Dan White went off the deep end and killed
you and Harvey. It was such a horrible moment. We had all
lived through so many of these moments—Kennedy, King,
Kennedy, Jonestown. I just wanted it all to stop.

Maybe everyone should have just let you re-appoint White.

You might have lost your re-election, but you and Harvey
would be old men today.

Sincerely,
Richie Ross

Michael Prokes
The People's Temple

Dear Michael,

I forgot that you killed yourself. I'm sorry.

I was watching an old PBS documentary about Jonestown, and at the end, there you were at the motel in Modesto where you committed suicide.

You looked so familiar to me. I remember the first time

we met. It was a year or so after your People's Temple crew helped elect George Moscone mayor of San Francisco. I was running Art Agnos' campaign for Assembly against Harvey Milk.

We were about the same age. And like a lot of guys we were looking to connect to something as the anti-war movement faded. I found it with Cesar Chavez. You went with Jim Jones. Maybe we had similar reasons.

I guess I was luckier than you.

I have to tell you that when you brought me in to have lunch with Rev. Jones, I had a really bad vibe. Even though all the politicians I was working for thought you guys were okay, I wasn't sure. I thought maybe it was just my old Catholic-grammar-school-nun-thing. They taught us it was a sin to even go into a church that wasn't Catholic.

You gave me a tour around People's Temple before we met Rev. Jones for lunch. When we were in the back room where you had a small clinic, one of your guys blurted out that this was where Rev. Jones cured people. He said some had cancer.

I caught your eye looking at me to see my reaction. You knew it was weird. I saw it in your face. I could tell you wanted to see if I thought it was weird, too.

I grew up in New York. My mom was a tough Brooklyn girl. When I left the seminary to come to California to work for Cesar, she gave me a last word of advice. "Richie, when you get out there, remember: only hang around regular people." Regular meant normal people.

No way was someone who cured cancer in a small room inside something called People's Temple "regular." And even though she wouldn't have thought Cesar Chavez was regular, he actually was and I felt it. Just like I felt Jim Jones wasn't when we sat down for lunch. He was wearing sunglasses. Inside.

We never did work together.

When the Jonestown massacre happened, I was rattled. I knew then that my mother was right and important politicians could be wrong. I never forgot it.

But I forgot you until the other night.

I want you to know that I don't judge you. We were all looking for something. You just found the wrong thing. Rest in peace, man.

Sincerely,
Richie Ross

Cresencio Trujillo
Dolores Hidalgo
Guanajuato, Mexico

Estimado Don Cresencio,

I am writing this as I sit in the middle of the plaza
in Dolores. Today is the 200th Anniversary of Mexican
Independence and I wanted your granddaughters to be
where they and Mexico were born.

I never told you how angry I was...after I risked everything to smuggle you into the United States...you only stayed a year and then you came back here.

As we waited for the festivities to begin when the clock would strike 11:00 p.m., I found myself noticing t-shirts. Of course, there were many red, white, and green shirts.

But here and there, I'd see "Lake Tahoe, California" or "Maui." There was a "Billabong," an "Iron Maiden." My favorite was "Andy's Liquor Store, Rochester New York."

The people wearing these shirts all had something in common. They had the look. You could see it. I could.

They had gone to "El Norte." Worked. Sent money home. Came home, carrying disappointment and a suitcase of things. The shirts on their backs with words about materially better lives...that never materialized.

As I looked at each face, I knew I had no right to judge why you or they would choose to leave or come home.

Richie Ross

Congressman Philip Burton
San Francisco, California

Dear Congressman Burton,

   I couldn't thank you before. I know you wouldn't
have wanted me to. In fact, you didn't want me to ever
acknowledge that what had happened, happened.
   Not sure if you remember me. I was only working for the
Assembly for six weeks when I got in trouble.

My mother-in-law had spent the winter in Mexico. She found her father-in-law, Cresencio Trujillo, very ill when she got there, and spent the whole winter nursing him back to health. He was 80-something.

Anyway, she made the mistake of thinking she could bring him to California. When she got to Tijuana things went bad. They didn't have enough money to pay for a coyote to smuggle him across and had to leave him in a motel in Tijuana.

I hatched the scheme that ended up getting me in trouble. I bought a dead man's green card from a buddy of mine's mother for $50. Then I loaded up the old Pontiac Grand Prix with lots of pottery and stuff to make it look like I had bought it all in Tijuana. Then my father-in-law, my wife, and I drove all night to Tijuana.

We got to the old motel where the old man was. We gave him his new green card. Then we headed back to the border crossing. Not much of a plan. We never even got our stories straight. And I never bothered to check the date of birth on the green card I bought. It was for a 60-year-old man. My passenger was way older than that. Shit.

We never made it through. They arrested us. I guess our lame and inconsistent stories convinced them we weren't pros. I said that my wife and I picked up the two men when they asked us for a ride. My father-in-law said that he met the old man at the motel they were staying at and the two of them asked us for a ride. My wife said she and her father asked me for a ride and then the old man kind of just tagged along. And the old man...he just refused to talk. He was sick.

They sent us back to Mexico and gave us a date with the U.S. Attorney in court.

The next morning we found a coyote, paid him half of his $300 fee, drove across the border and waited until midnight at the movie theater in Oxnard. He delivered the old man right on time.

On Tuesday, I told Art Agnos, who had hired me to work in Speaker McCarthy's operation, what I had done. He called you.

I was pretty nervous meeting you. I didn't even know much about you then. And I'm glad. Because if I did know, I would have been even more nervous.

Do you remember John Jacobs? He was a reporter back then at the *Examiner*. Anyway, he wrote this incredible book about you called *A Rage for Justice*. Maybe you'd be embarrassed to read it because it was so good, but man, it really lays out your history and all the gigantic things you did in your life and career.

When I walked into your office, you were on the phone. You had paper everywhere. And your hair was all messed up. You were big. And imposing. You pointed to a chair on the other side of your desk, so I sat down and waited while you stayed on the phone. I kept going over my story in my head, thinking about how I was going to explain what happened and why I thought I needed your help.

You hung up the phone and handed me a small piece of notepaper that had your name and Congress stuff on it. All you said was, "Here, go see this man in the immigration office on Sansome Street." That was it. I took the paper, looked at you, and knew that I was supposed to leave. I said, "Thank you." And left.

I went straight to Sansome Street and found my way to the man's office. He wasn't a big shot. I remember he had a very small office with a gray metal desk and piles of paper all around.

I handed him the paper and told him you sent me. He left his office for about a half hour. It seemed longer. Maybe it was. When he came back he just said he couldn't find any paperwork on me.

I looked at him for a moment. I was going to ask him what I should do next. Then my New York instincts kicked in...and I knew what he meant and I should just leave.

So, thanks.

I did a lot of work with your brother John. He ended up running for your old seat in the Assembly, then George's seat in the Senate, and he became the Senate president. He did a really good job. But was a pain in the ass sometimes. But mostly he was that way because he was pushing for really good things.

He helped me pass an important binding mediation law for the farm workers. And he did it from start to finish, no shit, in 54 minutes. Swear to God. I saved the time-stamped paperwork from when we got the bill language from Legislative Counsel. It was the last night of session. He dropped everything else he was doing and jammed the shit out of everyone. He moved the bill through committees and off the floors of both houses of the legislature in under an hour.

When your mom was dying, John was running for Assembly. He wanted to go visit with her. So I drove him over to the house in the Sunset. She was really sick. All around her bed were these incredible pictures of you, John, and Bob. Really historic pictures. You guys with presidents and civil rights leaders. It was a wonderful shrine to her three sons.

And you know how John is. He was crying when we left the house. I tried to give him something positive to think about, so I talked about all the pictures. John said something that has stuck with me ever since, "When you go, all you take are your memories."

Over the years, I've passed along my own version of that to my kids. I tell them life isn't a collection of things, it's a collection of days. So when you get up each day, look for a chance to add that day to your collection.

I always stayed loyal to John because of what you did for me.

It wasn't one of your big achievements. It won't be in the history books. But you saved my ass.

The Mexican girl I married in 1971 became a citizen in 2008 so she could vote for the first black president. Cool.

Sincerely,
Richie Ross

P.S. I made Sala's TV ads and helped her follow you into Congress. Nancy followed Sala and became the speaker of the House.

Leo McCarthy
Assembly Speaker

Dear Mr. Speaker,

   The other day I had dinner with Jerry Brown. He's running for governor again.
   I bet you've forgotten that my first official day on the Assembly payroll was the day he was sworn in as governor the first time.

I had worked in the Michael Wornum campaign for you, and afterward you had Art offer me a job. I didn't have a telephone. We were living in a terrible place over near 30th and Mission.

Every day, I would walk over to the Shell station with a bunch of quarters and call Art in your office from the pay phone. When we finally connected, he offered me the job. Eight hundred dollars a month and full medical. It was like going to heaven!

The first thing we did was move. The place we were in was so horrible. It was actually painted black inside. Everything. Walls. Ceiling. It was so flea-infested we never let the kids walk on the rugs.

We found a tiny, clean place over in Bayview-Hunters Point. It was in a garage. A guy took a two-car garage, put up a sheet rock wall, and made the apartment. It was nice. And $160 a month.

After we moved in, I went and bought a suit. I had seen a picture of you wearing a plaid suit. So that's what I bought. Neither of us would be caught dead in those now. No pun intended.

I took the Greyhound bus from San Francisco to the state Capitol. Just like you used to.

(Do you remember when you had your state car stolen? You were trying to catch the Greyhound and you were late. You pulled into the parking lot on Seventh and Mission and gave the guy the keys and ran for the bus. Unfortunately, the guy didn't work at the parking lot.)

Anyway, as the new kid on his first day in a real job, you arranged for me to sit in the public gallery right behind the members on the Assembly floor.

I don't remember who the two assemblymen were who sat right in front of me. But I was close enough to hear them talk to one another. When the chaplain was giving the invocation to begin the day, one of them says to the other, "We got to tell Leo to get rid of this asshole."

I was taken back. Geez.

That night when I got home, I was telling my wife all about my trip and the first day. Now, remember that at the time, she had only been in the country a couple of years. She was 23. She had no idea who you were, what the Assembly was, or where the Capitol was.

When I told her the story about what these assemblymen said about the chaplain, she didn't even look up from cooking. She just said, "Richie, these kind of people are going to hate you no matter what you do. So, if you're smart, you'll pick the reason."

To this day, that's the best advice anyone ever gave me in politics. I didn't realize it at the time. I didn't even understand it. But eventually I followed it. And it served me well.

Jerry looks good. He's in for a tough race. Not sure he can pull it off. But I gotta tell you his crazy ideas are better than the no-ideas government we've had.

I'll let you know how it turns out.

Richie

Miscarried Baby
Salinas, California

Dear Little One,

I'm sure that ever since you went to heaven 27 years ago, you've been looking down on your mom. I don't know her, but I hope she is doing okay.

From heaven, if you look to the northeast from Salinas, you'll see Sacramento. It's what we call the state Capital in

California.

I used to work there.

And that's where your very short life and mine touched each other.

Your mom was pregnant and working in the lettuce fields. Five of my wife's sisters were working with her.

The foreman who drove the bus that took them into the fields to work that day got confused and took them to the wrong field. It had just been poisoned with powerful stuff to kill bugs. But they didn't have a warning sign up.

After a couple of hours everyone started to get sick. They all ended up in the hospital. And that's where your mom had the miscarriage and why you didn't get born.

I used to be against politicians. But I ended up working for them because I needed a job. And after a while they convinced me, or I convinced myself, that working for them instead of protesting everything was the best way to make things better.

So when I heard about what happened to you, your mom, and my wife's sisters, I thought it would be simple to change the law so that farmers had to put up signs warning people to keep out of fields where there was poison.

There are two groups of people who get picked to work in the Capitol. One group is called the Democrats. They say they are for workers. The other group is called Republicans. They say they help businesses.

I had helped the Democrats get picked to be in the Capitol. So I went to each one of them to tell them what happened. They all told me how sorry they were to hear the news.

So then we wrote a new law.

But on the day when they met, all the rich farmers got together and said that the new law was bad because it would cost them money to put up the warning signs.

I wasn't worried. I was sure we would win.

When everyone finished talking, the chairman of the committee asked the other politicians if any of them wanted to approve the new law. None of them said anything. Not even any of the Democrats.

I walked out of the big room where they were meeting really angry and upset and disappointed.

I never really trusted any of them again. Because right then and there I saw that they really would only do things that helped people if it also helped them.

Part of me wanted to just walk out of the Capitol and never come back. But I was making too much money and I didn't.

I hope that heaven is as nice as everyone says. If you see a lady named Doris Ross tell her that her son, Richie, says hello and that I love her.

Sincerely,
Richie Ross

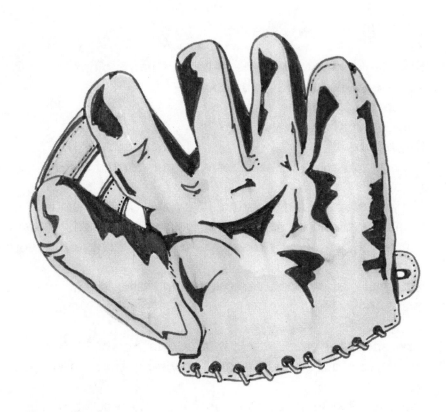

Mayor Lionel Wilson
Oakland, California

Dear Mr. Mayor,

I was up in Canada working on a hotel union campaign. I met this black lady who was a hotel housekeeper. Her name was Zeleda Davis.

When I introduced myself to her, I was struck by her accent. She told me she was originally from Jamaica.

"You from the U.S.?" she asked.

"Yes."

"Say, can you get me some of those Obama pins?"

"You mean his campaign buttons?"

"Yes, can you get me some?"

"Sure, how many do you want?"

"Oh, maybe 25 or 30."

I was curious. So I asked her why she wanted the buttons.

"They are for my lady friends. We have Obama parties."

"What do you do at your Obama parties?" I asked.

"Oh, we call all our friends in the U.S. and tell them to vote for Obama."

"Ms. Davis, is Obama's campaign important to black people all over the world?"

"Oh, yes."

"How about for you? Why is it important to you?"

"Oh, to see those two little girls playing in that big White House."

I watched President Obama throw out the first pitch at the all-star game. All of a sudden, you popped into my mind. Partly because I remembered you were the first black mayor of Oakland, but mostly because of baseball.

Man, I thought, this is something you'd have loved to see!

I remembered our last campaign together, sitting in your office in City Hall. You were telling me how, when you were a kid in Oakland, you had to swim in the estuary near the port because you couldn't go to the public pools.

Then, I noticed the old baseball glove you kept next to your desk. I asked you about it.

That's when I found out that you used to be a star player in the Negro League.

We talked about it for an hour. You became a completely different guy. Usually you were stiff and formal and pretty quiet.

You talked about when the team would get to the next town where you were going to play, how you would have to park the bus outside of town. How local black families would walk out to where the bus was and meet you guys. And how they would each take a player or two home with them, because you couldn't eat or sleep in any of the hotels down south.

I forget what position you told me you played.

Am I right that you were a lefty? The new president is. But he's a basketball player.

During his campaign he went over to Iraq (that's where we are at war) to visit the soldiers. He goes into the gym at the base, picks up a basketball, and shoots it from three-point range!

Gutsy. The whole TV world watching. Swish!

And his first pitch at the all-star game?

Well, let's just say he's a better president and better basketball player than he is a pitcher.

Take care,
Richie

Jess Unruh
Speaker of the Assembly
California State Treasurer

Dear Mr. Unruh,

   Willie Brown's Uncle Itzie said to be a good gambler you never bet all the money in your pocket; and you never try to win all the money you see.
   Pretty smart stuff.

Did it ever bother you that Willie broke your record for serving the longest of any speaker in California history?

It shouldn't. You gave up the job to run for governor against Ronald Reagan. And Willie kept the speakership by following Uncle Itzie's simple rule about gambling. Sure, once in a while he overplayed his hand. But most of the time he played it smart.

Anyway, here's a story about what happened when you died in office and what Willie did about getting you replaced.

Governor Wilson tried to appoint Dan Lungren to follow you as state treasurer. The once-nothing-much state treasurer job had become a powerhouse because of you. And everyone wanted it.

When the Senate refused to confirm Lungren, the whole thing went back up for grabs.

Willie started to push Tom Hayes. Remember Tom? He was the auditor general, nice guy and a Republican.

No one could figure out why Willie was pushing him.

I knew.

When Willie first became speaker, he named me chief administrative officer. I was the first political guy to get the job of running the Assembly.

Willie gave me a simple directive: "Ross, your job is to spend all the fucking money you can get your hands on to keep me speaker."

I did. We hired who the assemblymen wanted. We redecorated their offices. We bought new cars. We kissed their asses. Full-time. We kept them happy. You know.

But by April, I had spent the entire year's budget. We weren't going to make it to the beginning of the new fiscal year on July 1.

Tom was the auditor general. I found out he had a surplus of $2 million in his budget. I asked him if he'd "loan" the money to the Assembly. No one ever knew. And no one ever figured out why one of the most famous Democrats (you) was replaced by an unknown Republican.

No damage done. Two years later Jerry Brown's sister, Kathleen, beat Tom and became treasurer. But honestly, if Tom had won he would have done a good job.

Mr. Unruh, you were most famous for saying that "money was the mother's milk of politics." But it's not the most important thing I remember you saying....

You, Willie, and a bunch of his Assembly guys were all eating at the big corner table in Frank Fat's (no one goes there anymore). I walked by and you invited me to sit down. You were eating Frank's famous banana cream pie. You offered me a bite.

One of Willie's and your best buddies started shitting on me in front of everybody because of some election campaign we had barely won.

I couldn't say anything to defend myself. Willie would have killed me. And before long the whole lunch bunch was shitting on me.

You shut everyone up by putting your arm around me and telling me loud enough for them to hear, "A good rule in politics—I never ask my friends to like all my other friends."

When Michael Jordan retired from basketball, a sportswriter said that the best thing about Michael was how he respected his fans. "Michael never looked down on the people who looked up to him."

He could have written that about you.

Sincerely,
Richie Ross

"Don" Jaco
Lincoln, California

Dear Jaco,

    A couple of times in the last few years, my children have told me how much your story has meant to them.

    The country is in the middle of what they call the "Great Recession." Millions of people are losing their jobs and their homes.

But whenever I ask any of my kids if they are worried about it, your story always comes up.

As smart as you were, I don't think you know the story.

It was 1986. I had just lost three tough campaigns. My "reign" as "Willie Brown's Warlord" had come to an end.

I had five kids, a $400-something mortgage, and $600 in the bank.

A few hours before I left my office in the Capitol for the last time, I got a telephone call.

It was from a guy named Ethan Wagner.

Ethan was older than me. But he had held the same job I had for a previous speaker named Bob Moretti. Ethan was Bob's top gun. But when Moretti ran and lost for governor in 1974, Ethan was out.

Ironically, his last day in the Assembly was my first day.

He opened his own consulting and lobbying business. And was very successful. Whenever I would see him, I would call him "Mr. Wagner." Not out of any phony respect. But just because he was older.

Eventually, Ethan moved to New York.

He called me from there.

"Richie, this is Ethan Wagner. I'm just calling to tell you there are two kinds of people in politics. Before last Tuesday's elections, you thought it was Democrats and Republicans. And since last Tuesday, you've been thinking that it's winners and losers. I just wanted to call and say the two kinds of people in politics are long-termers and short-timers. And you get to choose. Have a good day."

That was it. I thanked him for the call. And he said goodbye.

So driving home that evening, I headed to the bird shop over on Fulton Avenue. I went in and asked the lady if she knew which bird my wife and kids had been coming by to look at.

She showed me.

So I bought you and brought you home. Determined not to quit or ever be afraid of losing.

The kids all named you. "Jaco" came from something they read about how Portuguese sailors first started catching African Grey parrots. Everyone laughed whenever you shouted something. They said it made you the boss, so they added "Don."

Maya and Diego buried you on the ranch. R.I.P.

R.

Mr. Jack Henning
California Federation of Labor, AFL-CIO
San Francisco, California

Dear Mr. Henning,

    You were the most honorable man I ever met in politics.
    I don't know why you picked me to run the campaign for
Labor's initiative to restore worker safety programs when
the Republicans had shut down Cal-OSHA. Right before the

interview started, I got a call. My mother had died. I was stunned. Didn't know whether to cry or not.

Couldn't cry. After my last visit to see her a few months before, I had cried it all out. I was sitting in the Newark airport waiting for my plane. All of a sudden I just broke down. In front of strangers. A lady came up to me and asked me if there was something she could do.

So sitting there in front of you and the other labor union leaders, I couldn't really "perform." I blew the interview.

You followed me out the room. You asked me what was wrong. I told you. You said you were sorry.

I flew to New York that night with my brother John.

A week or so later, you called me and asked me if I still wanted to do the campaign.

You knew that I had lost my job in Willie's office. I needed the work. You gave me the chance.

I loved working with you on that campaign. You were such a powerful public speaker. You believed so deeply in what we were trying to do.

Our campaign ran short of money at the end. A lot of labor leaders didn't keep their commitments. You went and borrowed $50,000 against your house in San Francisco.

No one does that. No one.

That either makes almost everyone else a phony or it makes you extraordinary.

Thanks for being such a fine man.

Sincerely,
Richie Ross

Senator Ralph Dills
State Capitol
Sacramento, California

Dear Senator,

Your hair was blue. Mine was long. You looked at me. I looked at you. The difference in our ages was 40 years.

As we talked, I wasn't listening as much as I was wondering. Your wide tie with the racehorse tie clip. The

99

plaid sport coat. The cans of Coca-Cola on your desk. How was this going to work? How was I supposed to get you re-elected?

I didn't know what to say to you that first day. But I noticed a really thick bound book on your desk. You told me it was about you, a part of the State Library's "Living History" project. Man, I thought to myself, that must be some pretty boring shit.

I ran out of things to say pretty quick. Especially after I asked you what your greatest achievements were in the Legislature and you told me you "abolished the sales tax on chicken."

I looked back at the book. Faking it, I asked, "Could I take it to read?"

You were flattered.

I read it.

I came back the next week.

In 1943, you had been expelled from the Assembly—booted out, stripped of office—because you refused to vote for some law attacking Japanese-Americans.

When I asked you about it at our second meeting, you didn't give me a speech.

You just explained how a Japanese-American couple had helped you get through state teachers' college and how you visited them in the internment camp and why you didn't care what the Republicans did to you.

I was embarrassed. For myself. For judging the book by the cover.

After that, it was all you and me. And it was fun. We flew. Defying gravity. It was the beginning of the "term limits era." And you had first been elected in 1932.

I still laugh about how the two of us decided that the George Burns model for "cool" was how you'd win.

Hey, you know what—your obituary stories used our

campaign slogan, "Too old to quit." That was cool.

Senator, I've had a lot of interesting opportunities. One of them was helping Indian tribes in California win the right to operate gaming on their lands.

No one remembers. Success has so many fathers. But it was one day, on one vote, that you changed everything for them.

You'd been a loyal guy to the card rooms and racetracks. You chaired the Senate committee that handled gambling. Those guys had supported you for years.

Right after your re-election, there was a bill in your committee. The tribes had no power. They needed your vote. The card rooms and racetracks were all on the other side. I was working for the Indian tribes.

Other lobbyists for tribes made it clear that "Richie is Dills' guy. He re-elected him." They knew it would be impossible for me to persuade you to side with the Indians against the card rooms and racetracks. They were just fucking me.

I went up to your office five minutes before the 9:00 committee hearing was to start. Do you remember?

"Young man, what can I do for you?"

"Senator, I made you look good last year."

"You did indeed. You did indeed."

"Senator, I will be in your committee this morning sitting with some people. You could sure make me look good today."

"Understood."

You walked into the hearing room. Took your gavel. The hearing room gasped as you voted with the tribes that morning. The other Democrats just followed your lead.

Nothing has been the same for the tribes since. No one remembers any of this anymore. History is easily dismissed. Years later, the younger tribal leaders didn't keep me around. Didn't see my value.

I'm the last person who can fault them for that. I almost did the same thing to you.

Sincerely,
Richie

John Lennon
New York City

Dear John,

My son Joaquin and I were producing a television commercial for a children's hospitals bond campaign in California. Yoko let us use "Imagine" for the ad!
That was so great of her.
We didn't use the whole song. The ad was only 30 seconds

long. But we had all these kids with serious illnesses singing, "Imagine all the people, sharing all the world. You may say that I'm a dreamer, but I'm not the only one."

You would have loved it!

Sadly, some of the parents decided not to let their kids be in the commercial. They were offended by some of the other lyrics. The ones that bothered them the most was "Imagine there's no heaven …" and "Imagine there's no countries, nothing to kill or die for and no religions too."

I understood.

They were really nice people. And even I could remember wincing back when I first heard the "no religions too" line.

I keep a photo in my office of the billboard you and Yoko bought on Times Square. The one that said "War is Over...If You Want."

Sadly, we are still at war. Not in Vietnam. But in Iraq and Afghanistan. And worse yet, it's a "religious" war.

Some religious nut-jobs thought that flying hijacked planes into the World Trade towers was a way to get to "heaven."

But you imagined all that. The rest of us didn't.

Sincerely,
Richie Ross

Jack Killea
San Diego, California

Dear Jack,

   Did you have anything to do with Che Guevara being killed?
   Bill Cavala and I always wondered. I think Bill finally decided it would make a good story to tell people that you were.

You and Lucy were two of the first three people hired to work for the CIA. You both were assigned to the American Embassy in Mexico City when Che was killed.

Anyway, we enjoyed speculating.

When Lucy was running the first time you tried to give us a lot of information you had about her opponents. You gave us credit card receipts, phone bills, cancelled checks.

"Jesus Christ, Jack," I said, "we can't use this stuff. We aren't supposed to have it. It's illegal. We could never explain how we got it. And shit, we don't need it."

Didn't stop you. Two years later another opponent, another envelope. Was it after the third time that you finally stopped?

Your network of retired military spooks in San Diego must have been something. I probably met some of them at your funeral. But they weren't going to introduce themselves to me as old spies.

Lucy had me give the eulogy. She knew that I knew something very special about you.

I didn't save what I wrote. I wish I had. But what I talked about was how lucky I'd been to learn about being a husband by watching you.

I remember asking you about how it felt to have Lucy starting her political career at age 60. You were older.

"It's her turn." That's all you said.

You did the campaign bookkeeping, gave us insights and news stories you tore out of the *New York Times*, and kept us all in honest, earnest pursuit of what was best for Lucy.

You showed us all how a man could take a backseat without having a chauffeur or being a loser. And do it with love and grace.

The only other man I've known who stayed married for over 50 years was Salvador Plascencia.

He was an immigrant from Mexico. Big family. A success, like you. But different. A baker.

At his 50th wedding anniversary his family had a big party
at the Holiday Inn in Sacramento. I was drinking beer with a
few of his sons-in-law. (My wife and I are godparents to one
of the granddaughters, so we are part of the family.)

One of the guys saw "Don" Plascencia sitting with his
hands folded in his lap. He looked nice in a suit. I had never
seen him in one. Anyway, my compadre Chema says, "Fifty
years. How did he do it?"

"I'll ask him," I said. They all laughed and told me I
couldn't, shouldn't. I did. "Señor Plascencia, we all want to
know your secret. How did you stay married for fifty years?"

Mr. Plascencia looked up and answered in Spanish. "I get
up every morning around 4:00. I have my coffee and then I
go to my bakery. I work all day until around 3:00, sometimes
a little later. I drive home. I eat a little supper. I sit in my
chair and watch some television. After a little while, I fall
asleep. Then I go to bed."

We all listened. We waited.

Mr. Plascencia gave us the hint of a smile. And said,
"Seven days a week."

I think the truth about marriage is in both your "It's her
turn" and Mr. Placencia's "Seven days a week."

Marriage is about taking turns and staying steady.

We move through stages in a marriage. First there's
passion with all the heat—both good and bad.

Then there's tolerance, when we just kind of get through it
and mumble under our breath—never loud enough so she'll
hear.

And finally comes appreciation, where you accept who you
are and who you're married to and what you're never going
to change or try to change anymore. And how you just want
them to have what they want, even if you don't want what
they want. And they do the same.

Thanks so much. I do appreciate what an honor it was to know you.

Sincerely,
Richie

Joe Serna
Sacramento, California

Dear Joe,

Jesus, Joe. What were we thinking? We thought we were such slick pros. Big shot mayor. Big shot sidekick.

Steve Thompson got Bob Matsui who got Vice President Gore's help to see if we could "juice" you into some experimental cancer drug treatment thing at UCLA.

You had lost 80 pounds, so I had Mike the Greek tailor

come over to the house and re-cut your best suit to fit. I had the barber come. Angelo got us a private jet. The sheriff sent a car. We thought we had it all going on.

We laughed about what a great play we were making.

Remember when I walked you into UCLA Medical Center? You asked me, "How do I look, compadre?" "You look great, Joe." Great hair cut. Nice suit. Good friend.

We get into the doctor's office and the first thing they do is make you take your clothes off. Bad scene. Political cover-ups rarely work.

You didn't make it into the program, but we laughed so hard, I thought you were going to croak on the plane ride home.

I told Biba the truth about the pork chops. She is a great lady. She knew you were too sick to eat them, but she prepared them as though they were for the Queen of England. She laughed when I explained how much you loved them, but you'd get yelled at by your wife if you got caught cooking them. Why'd you marry a vegetarian? When I brought them over to you, you smiled. Cancer took away your appetite, but not your sense of smell.

Joe, you died the way I want to.

Boots on.

I'll never forget you, on your deathbed, making calls to make things happen.

You endorsed friends running for office. You shifted all your campaign money to help the farm workers. And you got even with the city cop union for double-crossing you in the last campaign.

They had the contract to provide security at the arena for all the NBA games. It was a plum assignment to make extra money watching the games.

But the sheriff wanted you and me to help get the contract shifted to his department so his guys could get the gig. The

Maloofs were the new owners and their guy, John Thomas was a good guy.

I was sitting on your bed when the phone rang.

You answered and listened. And then you said, "I'll talk to Richie."

When you hung up, I asked you what was happening.

"That was the city manager. He wants me to get you to stop messing around with the cops' deal at the arena. I told him I'd talk to you."

Then you grinned, "And I just did."

Your body might have been lame but you never were a lame duck. Great move.

Your funeral was bigger than anything we ever had when you were alive. It's like a law of physics in politics. Cathedrals half full of people sad to see you go...and the other half with people glad to see you go.

You did better than a 50-50 split.

Love,
Richie

Tiny LaChappa
Barona Indian Reservation
San Diego, California

Dear Vice-Chairman LaChappa,

When you first started telling me about tribal sovereignty, I thought you were crazy.

You thought I was just white.

Turns out your craziness wasn't so crazy. I'm still just white. But a little wiser.

Our first week together. Going around the country. Sitting behind one-way glass watching ordinary Americans talk about "sovereignty" on Indian lands. It opened your eyes. But it closed my mind.

The guy in Chicago who said "sovereignty" was "money in England." The woman in New York—"Yeah, so we stole the land from them. So what. They probably stole it from someone else."

I never believed it would happen, but it actually has. People kind of get what it means. And they don't think it's bizarre, or anti-American. And I'm so happy you lived to see it begin.

When you and Chairman Pico got back from fighting in Vietnam, Anthony told me how you both went down a pretty bad path. Raising hell. Drinking a lot.

Somehow, you both became these very religious guys in a way. You spoke plainly. Anthony poetically.

The best thing I ever heard Chairman Pico say was after our first tough political campaign together. We lost. Remember? We tried to defeat the Republican state attorney general. It was the first big political move the tribes ever had made in California.

So Anthony called everyone together. He wanted a big discussion. But he didn't say anything. He just listened.

Afterward, I asked him why he didn't talk.

He told me that you don't catch coyotes by chasing them. You stay still. Act wounded. The coyote will come to you.

Anthony watched. He listened. He figured out who he could trust and who just wanted the tribes' money.

The best thing I ever heard you say was that night in Sacramento, when some of the other tribes' advisors accused me of making some anti-Indian racial statements. It was late at night in the hotel across the street from the Capitol. And I was "on trial" in front of 20 or so tribal leaders.

After everyone was done speaking, you stood up. And all you said was you didn't believe my accusers. You believed me. You sat down. And the meeting ended. And we went on to do some good things for many good people.

I didn't come to your funeral. I've only gone to a couple in my life. And I wish I could have skipped those. I like to think that people I've known and loved are still alive. Because they are. To me.

Peace,
Richie

Johnnie Cochran
Los Angeles, California

Dear Mr. Cochran,

Five years after "If it doesn't fit, you must acquit," I got sued by a politician buddy of Willie Brown's after a very hard-hitting campaign that beat him by seven votes.

The guy was a sore loser. He sued me for libel. It went all the way to the state Supreme Court. I won.

He went to the press and called me "the Johnnie Cochran of Democratic politics." He didn't mean it as a compliment.

But I was flattered.

Here's why I love Willie Brown. Willie was pissed off that I was against his candidate. When I saw the quote, I thought it was a great way to let Willie know that he supported the wrong guy.

So I took the article with the quote comparing me to you and sent it to Willie with a little note that simply asked if he would ask you to autograph it for me. No explanation. He is so smart he wouldn't need one.

No disrespect to you, but I was a lot more interested in sending Willie a message than I was in getting your autograph.

Six months later—six months—I get a manila envelope in the mail.

There's the article with your autograph. You signed it right over the quote "Richie Ross is the Johnnie Cochran of Democratic politics." No note from Willie.

It was his way of saying, "Got the message."

I framed it and hung it in my office.

Sincerely,
Richie Ross

P.S. O.J. ended up in jail anyway. He got busted in some Las Vegas hotel in an argument over some of his "memorabilia." So in the end, the glove didn't fit but the shoe did, and he had to wear it.

שלום

Chandra Levy
Washington, D.C.

Dear Ms. Levy,

Your death was an unspeakable horror for all the people who loved you. Watching your mom over the many months that they searched for you was terrible.

My daughter was living in Georgetown while all this was happening. She was about your age. I can't imagine the terror your family endured.

Sadly, the press decided to turn whatever relationship you may have had with Gary into the basis for serializing the tragedy.

I've known Gary for 30 years. I helped him get elected to the Legislature. And handled his re-election campaigns for Congress.

Including the last one.

Gary was a good public official. He did a lot of good things. And even though he represented Modesto, the home base for the Gallos, Gary helped me settle some very difficult contracts between them and the United Farm Workers.

I wanted you to know that I stuck with him after your death and before it finally came out that he had nothing to do with it.

Please know, I never believed he had anything to do with your murder. As for the allegations about his relationship with you, I don't think it's my place to judge people's private lives.

I have known many, many young people who have come into politics and government to make a difference in the world. Just like you. Like I used to be.

I stuck with Gary because I didn't want to be a phony. His "friends" not only jumped off the bandwagon, they jumped at the chance to throw him under the bus.

I hated being on George Stephanopoulos' Sunday morning news show trying to answer, "How are you possibly going to re-elect Congressman Gary Condit?" I didn't have a good answer then. And the voters picked someone else.

Sincerely,
Richie Ross

Pete the Cotton Farmer
Sundown, Texas

Dear Pete,

I just got back from Sundown. It was quite a trip.

I married Simón and Carmen's oldest girl. Your daughter, Kate, used to have all their girls sit down, like her audience, while Kate sang to them.

The girls always wondered if Kate became a singer.

I took my wife back to Sundown as a surprise. As you can imagine, the place where you live from age 6 to 13 is the place with your most magical memories.

She wanted to find your farm. Was the house she lived in still there?

We had no address. But Sundown hasn't grown. How hard could it be?

Our hotel was in Lubbock. We landed late on a Friday afternoon in July. But she was so anxious she asked me to head straight to Sundown. She posed for a picture under the "Welcome to Sundown" sign on the road.

Cotton fields with oil derricks. As far as you can see. No restaurants open after 2:00 in the afternoon. A couple of small stores. We bought an old rusty Texas star that I keep on my desk as a paperweight. Quiet side streets where strangers get noticed. We drove down each one.

The school was there. It was as my wife remembered it. She brought her yearbook. She saves stuff. She was in second grade. Kate was in fifth.

We drove back to Lubbock after dark, confident we'd find your farm the next day.

I knew the family's story of how they crossed the Rio Grande. How her dad, Simón, carried each of the girls across the river one by one. And how Carmen and the baby slipped in the water and nearly drowned. And how they all made it.

They walked for the next two days and nights. Staying away from the roads.

Simón would build a fire all around where they slept each night to keep the snakes away. And the only water they could drink was green and smelly.

Simón had a car hidden. They finally got to it. And they drove to Sundown.

I've always heard how nice you were. Simón irrigated all your cotton. Do you remember my wife? I bet she was the first 6-year-old you ever saw drive your old pickup.

She told me how she would drive across the wide-open spaces while her dad sat on the hood of the truck with his rifle. They'd kill rabbits to eat.

I know you didn't pay them more than a few dollars a day. But I also know you worked as hard as they did and you didn't have any money yourself.

The girls hated the government food the ladies from the church would bring to the poor families. Big pieces of cheese and powdered milk. But they loved all the food they grew in their garden and their mom canned for the winter. They kept it all in the basement. And they'd have to hide down there when tornado season came.

Saturday we headed back to Sundown.

I remembered how the girls described running down a long dirt driveway when the school bus was coming. They could see the bus coming over the crest of a hill. So the first thing we looked for was a hill.

I wouldn't call anything we found a hill. There were places where the land rose a little. They were all on the northwest side of town. So we just drove up and down and side to side on every road. We were both looking. She was talking. I was listening.

At lunchtime, we saw this Mexican family with a grill and a sign and a picnic table in their dirt front yard. We pulled in for lunch.

We took her yearbook and opened it to the fifth grade page and asked the ladies who were cooking if they knew who Kate was. They didn't. But they pointed to the house next door and told us that the family there had been in Sundown for *muchos años*.

Sure enough. In fact, there were only two other little Mexican kids in the yearbook and one of them lived in this house. But he wasn't home.

The people who were home kind of told us where Kate's family used to live. We were so excited. We thanked them and hurried off.

We followed the directions. But your house was gone. A small development of brick houses was where your farm used to be.

We headed back for Lubbock. A little disappointed.

As we left town, there was an irrigation company on the left side of the road. It was late Saturday afternoon and a couple of guys were standing next to the company trucks in the parking lot.

I pulled in. They'd know every farm.

"Excuse me, do either of you know an old farming family here? The man's name was Pete."

They didn't know you. But they said there was a guy inside who might.

Turns out, your son ran this irrigation business up until he retired two years ago! What luck.

Your son moved away. The guys didn't know where but they thought Kate moved to Dallas many years ago and that your son probably went there, too.

Talking to someone who knew someone who knew you... it was like "proof of life" in the movies. The little girl who remembered you really did live here and all that she remembered was true and not a dream.

Sincerely,
Richie Ross

P.S. The whole family remembers that after the "*migra*" deported them, you came all the way to Mexico to vouch for them so they could return to America with their papers.

Chicken Man
Yuba City, California

Dear Sir,

   I am the father of the two little kids who put you out of business.
   The first time we took Diego and Maya to the flea market to sell their chickens, you walked up to our car and told us you'd buy them all right away for $5.00 each.

Frankly, I was ready to sell them to you.

My wife said no.

She wanted the kids to learn how to sell them.

Right away, we saw all the Hmong ladies. They were walking from car to car looking at the chickens people were selling.

You kept interrupting them and buying all the scrawny chickens up before the Hmong ladies could. Then you were turning around and selling them for $7.00.

It was a piss-off.

So my wife sent my little girl over to the ladies to tell them we had really fat chickens and that they could buy them for $5.00. In about a few minutes all the chickens were gone. The kids could hardly keep up taking the money and putting the chickens in old feedbags. We sold about 50 of them that day.

My wife just stared at you as we drove away.

Then she said we were going to come back every week and do the same thing until we put you out of business. And we did.

It took us a year and more than a thousand chickens. And two little 5- and 6-year-old kids learned more than just how to catch their chickens and sell their chickens—they learned that it isn't good to let people take advantage of other people just because they couldn't speak English or were from another country.

And that made all those Saturdays worth it to me...even though I hated smelling those chickens in our car.

Sincerely,
Richard Ross

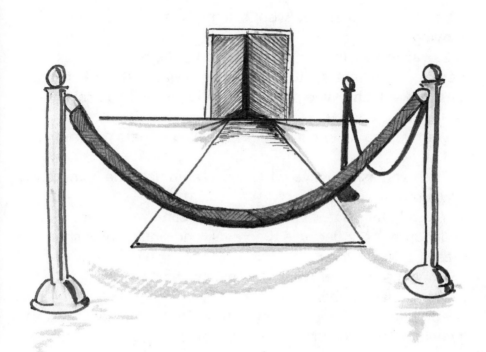

Angel the Elevator Guy
World Trade Center

Dear Angel,

I hope you don't get this letter. I hope you're still alive.
You won't remember me. But you might remember my
daughter. Her name is Maya. When you met her she was
around 14.
We were on the elevator line to go up to the top of the

World Trade Center. You were the guy keeping the line moving.

It was Maya's first time in New York. She had that look on her face. You spotted it. You asked her where she was from. She told you she lived on a ranch in California. You said you always wanted to go to "Frisco."

We told you no one in California called it that. You said you did.

Then you asked Maya if the city scared her. She admitted shyly that it did.

You told her that she shouldn't be wearing a camera around her neck because then everyone would know she wasn't a New Yorker.

Do you remember what you told her next?

We still laugh about it.

You told her, "Keep your eyes to yourself. You don't look at people in the eye in New York. 'Cause then they're going to ask you, what are you looking at? And that'll start something you don't want to start."

She nodded at you and turned to me. I shrugged my shoulders and told her, "See."

I was pretty amazed that a young Puerto Rican kid like you had been taught the same thing by your mother that I'd been taught by mine a long time before.

Our moms probably had nothing else in common.

When we were on the subway coming to the World Trade Center that day, I had told Maya and her brother, Diego, the same thing. "Keep your eyes to yourself." They thought I was nuts. Or just kidding.

I hope you either got a different job or got out before the shit happened.

Richie from California

-92' Suzuki-

Victor
Salinas, California

Dear Victor,

Your murder hasn't been solved. I don't think it will be.
There were a record number of drug- and gang-related
murders in Salinas again this year. There's no way the cops
can keep up with this madness.

Your aunt and I knew you were in trouble when you

showed up out of the blue at the ranch.

Of course, you were welcome. We didn't need you to explain why you needed to be there. We watched how tough it was on you. We could see you were strung-out on some kind of drugs.

But to your credit you toughed it out.

I'm sure you thought we were going to kill you the way we had you working on the ranch. We were trying to help you "sweat it out." All the drugs in your body.

I don't know what it is about your mom's whole family, but all the girls believe "sweating it out" will cure everything. Makes me laugh. I'm always being put through some kind of sweating-it-out... sweating out the coffee I drink, the cigarettes I smoke. The best is when they give us tequila to sweat out a cold. Ahhh!

But you have to admit, after about a month you were in pretty good shape.

Hey, remember that little Suzuki car you fixed and got running? Your aunt still drives it all around the ranch. She took out all the seats. And has it packed with tools and irrigation sprinklers and stuff for the cattle. It's really funny. She even took out the driver's seat and put a big log that she sits on. Who knows? It's her thing.

We both regret that you didn't stay with us longer.

I should have done more for you.

Love,
Uncle Richie

Dear Mom,

The only time any of us—me, Rob, John, Frank, or Dave—ever bring you up, it's always to laugh.

All your sayings—"Take an aspirin." "You're such a horse's ass." "Don't be a sissy Mary Agnes." "I'm chilly, put a sweater on."

We enjoy those moments today as much as we always enjoyed them with you.

I don't keep any pictures of you, Mom. I know how much you hated pictures of yourself. And I sure as hell know that you would have killed Dad, if you could have, when he had your casket open at the wake. I was pissed off at him, too. I heard you tell him over and over that you didn't want that.

But the other reason I don't keep a picture is that I don't need one. Because I always hear you talking to me.

I remember Rob and me saying Hail Marys so the Studebaker would start when the Brooklyn Ferry got back to Staten Island. And you know what, Mom? I do say Hail Marys when the kids are having a tough time. I guess I still think, or hope, they work. But every time I do, I think of you.

Hail Marys and aspirin were the same for you. They're small. You can take them anywhere. And they can take care of anything.

There's a lot of good things I could say to you, but I guess I just don't feel like I need to. You and me used to write to each other all the time.

The one thing I want you to know is that your teaching me how to fight and defend myself and my family has really been important.

I can still taste the piss from those kids in the housing projects who held me down and took turns pissing on me. And I still remember you making me go back outside to punch them in the face. And I still remember getting three stitches after they hit me back.

But you know, you were right. Stitches or not.

Esperanza got married on the ranch. We all worked for weeks rebuilding an old falling-down barn way in the back and we turned it into the coolest wedding chapel you can imagine. It was a great project. And one we'll always remember doing together.

Mom, I am really sorry I came to see you that last time. You were right. I shouldn't have.

It's one thing to hear that you were getting close to dying and in a lot of pain, and another to actually see it.

I know it took guts for you to let them take you off the

morphine so that you'd be able to see us. But Jesus Christ. What were we thinking? The last thing you ever said to me in the middle of all your anguished screams was, "I didn't want you to see me like this."

Fortunately, I don't hear your voice saying that often. And when I do I can wipe it out by hearing you calling me "such a horse's ass" for my hippie clothes and long hair. And how we would eat pizza sitting on your bed when you were sick, and how we'd laugh and tell sacrilegious jokes right in front of your Blessed Mother statue.

This will amaze you: a year after you died I was working in Hawaii. A great couple there, Herb and Carroll Takahashi, had gotten me into a political campaign. On a Friday or Saturday evening, they told me they were taking me to a "bon dance" at a Buddhist temple.

It's this really cool event. They build like a 20-foot-high wooden platform and there are these guys who are drummers on top. Everyone dances around the platform in a big circle. You can dance as much as you want; the drumming never seems to stop, and people come in and out of the circle whenever they want. There's food being sold and sodas.

It was cool. The drumming beats are great. And people of every age are all dancing in this big circle, smiling and talking to each other.

I saw this table where they were selling these little rafts with a candle on them. So I asked Herb and Carroll what they were for.

They explained it was a tradition for people who had had a loved one die during the last year to buy one, and then later in the evening everybody would bring their raft down to the ocean. Anyway, I bought one for you. Didn't think it would be a big deal.

A couple of hours later, the Buddhist priest started to

gather everyone because it was getting to be the time when the tides would be right. After everyone was paying attention, he started some prayers and led everyone a few hundred feet to the beach behind the church.

At the edge of the beach, everyone who had a raft lit the candle on it and then people started to put them in the water. It was dark, but the moon was out. Suddenly, there were hundreds of these little rafts with candles on them all slowly going out to sea. And the people were praying. And the drummers were drumming.

I kept my eye on your raft as long as I could. I had tears. And after a while your candle and all the other candles got so small that I couldn't tell which one was you.

Everything else is fine. Will be good. Will see you soon enough.

Love,
Richie

Dear Joaquin, Esperanza, Diego, and Maya,

Don't worry. You're not dead.

I've given each of you a lot of advice. Some of it good. Some of it maybe not.

But I'm sure about this...

Write letters like these. They don't have to become a book. The people you write to don't have to be famous. They don't have to be friends.

When I started to write these letters, I realized that each person I wrote to was important. As I wrote to them, I found myself really writing to them...as though they were alive. In the moment, they really were.

The process you'll go through will make you reflect on the value of people you meet, know, work with, fight with, love or not.

You'll appreciate your own value as you recognize the value in those you'll encounter in life's journey.

When my life is over, I'd love to get a letter from you.

Love,
Dad

About the Author

Richie Ross, a former Catholic seminarian and anti-Vietnam War activist, has been a political consultant for 36 years. He has been involved in hundreds of campaigns at every level of government. A former chief of staff for California's legendary Assembly Speaker Willie Brown, Ross has worked as a union organizer for the United Farm Workers and a strategist for the hotel workers' union. He has been married for 39 years and has four children.

To post your letters to dead people visit www.myletterstodeadpeople.com.

LaVergne, TN USA
06 April 2011
223216LV00002B/31/P

9 781935 953111